Piano • Vocal • Guitar

bethanydillon

ISBN 0-634-08279-5

HAL•LEONARD®
CORPORATION
7777 W. BLUEMOUND RD. P.O. BOX 13819 MILWAUKEE, WI 53213

Visit Hal Leonard Online at
www.halleonard.com

contents

REVOLUTIONARIES

Words and Music by
BETHANY DILLON

GREAT BIG MYSTERY

Words and Music by BETHANY DILLON
and ED CASH

Air is dry, the sun is gone; ___ when I breathe, I breathe a - lone. ___

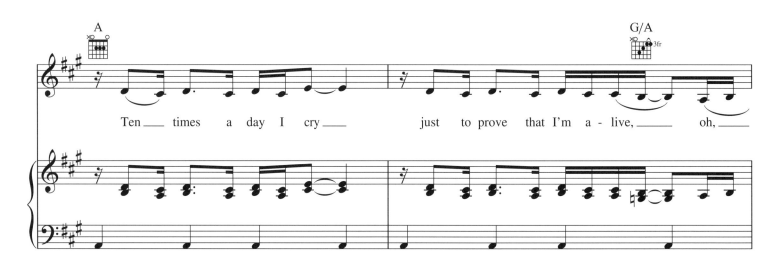

Ten ___ times a day I cry ___ just to prove that I'm a - live, ___ oh, ___

BEAUTIFUL

Words and Music by BETHANY DILLON
and ED CASH

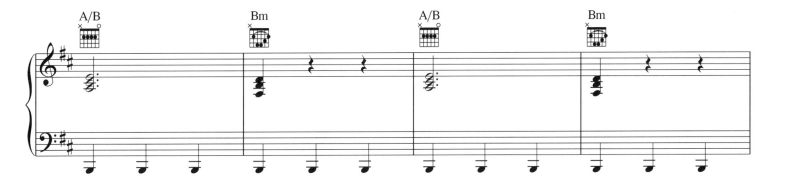

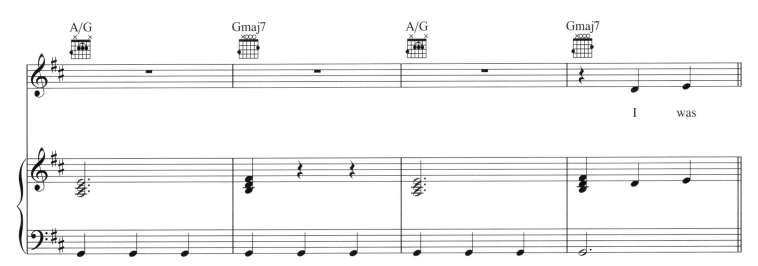

Recorded a half step lower.

Beau - ti - ful. _____
(Vocal 1st time only)

Optional Ending

Repeat and Fade

MOVE FORWARD

Words and Music by
BETHANY DILLON

FOR MY LOVE

Words and Music by
BETHANY DILLON

Moderate Rock beat

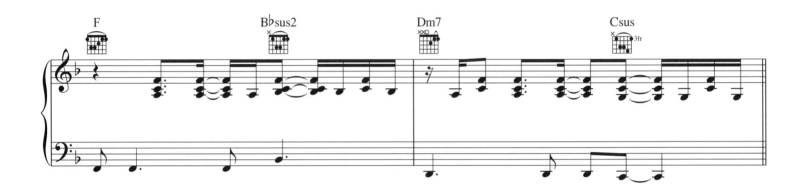

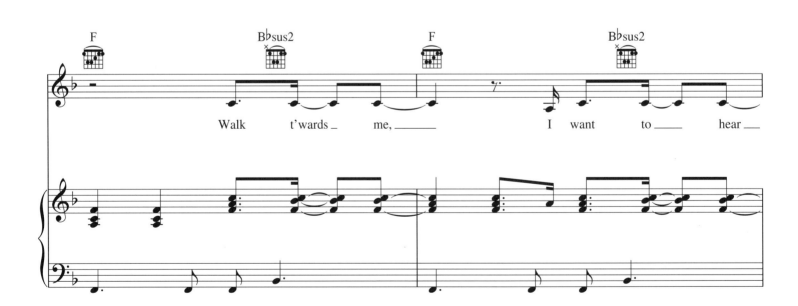

Walk t'wards __ me, _____ I want to __ hear __

D.S. al Coda

there I want to be ___ pur - sued. ___

CODA

me for my love. ___ A dream I won't wake __

___ from, ___ a sto - ry that will

nev - er ___ end. ___ The ground your feet walk __

44

ALL I NEED

Words and Music by BETHANY DILLON,
ED CASH and DAVE BARNES

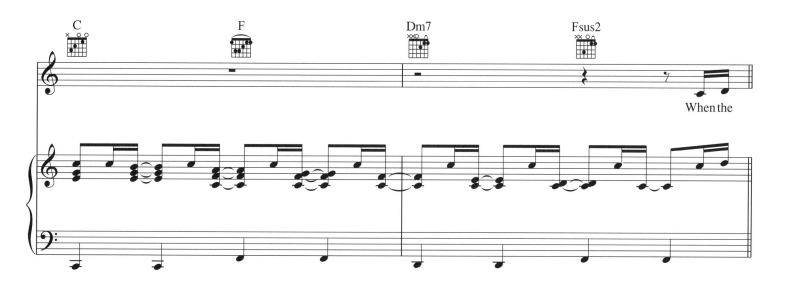

When the

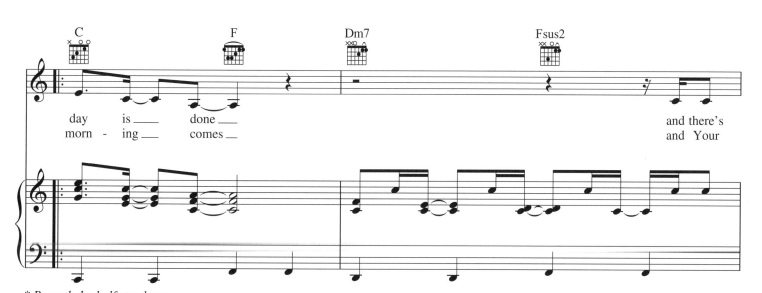

day   is ___   done ___   and there's
morn - ing ___   comes ___   and Your

Recorded a half step lower.

You fill me _____ when ___ I'm emp-

-ty. There is noth - ing else; ___ You're ___ all I _____ need. ___

When the

AIMLESS

Words and Music by BETHANY DILLON
and ED CASH

Moderately slow

The cur-tain falls, _ down ___ she goes. So long, _ worth. _____

* Recorded a half step lower.

To Coda

LEAD ME ON

Words and Music by MICHAEL W. SMITH,
WAYNE KIRKPATRICK and AMY GRANT

Recorded a half step lower.

EXODUS

Words and Music by BETHANY DILLON
and ED CASH

Come, come, fall - en ones, dance
flect, re - flect on all your days; you

in the heal - ing stream. He has faith - ful - ly kept
weren't so free then. Once you were all

70

God is faith - ful, _____ our God is faith - ful."

WHY

Words and Music by BETHANY DILLON
and JOSHUA MOORE

A VOICE CALLING OUT

Words and Music by
BETHANY DILLON

Very freely

With excitement, in one

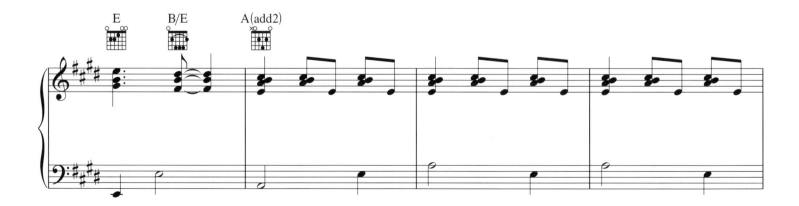

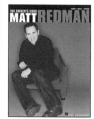